Dentists Are No Big Deal © 2023 by Debbie Kesslering and Ashley Vercammen. All rights reserved.

Published by Home Style Teachers. www.ashley-vercammen.ca.

All rights reserved. This book contains material protected under international and federal copyright laws and treaties. Any unauthorized reprint or use of this material is prohibited. No part of this book may be reproduced or transmitted in any form or by any means, electronic or mechanical, including photocopying, recording, or by any information storage and retrieval system without express written permission from the author.

Identifier: ISBN: 978-1-7781529-8-6 (paperback)

Dedication Page

I have had the opportunity to work with many World Class Dental Therapists, Dentists, Hygienists and Assistants. I would like to dedicate this book to my fellow 'sugar bug catchers'!!

-Debbie Kesslering

"Good morning, Nora!" said, Dad. "Today is a special day. We will go to the dentist to get your teeth checked".

"And it's no big deal," said Nora. "You're right!" said dad.

"Well," said Dad. "We need to look for sugar bugs."
"Remember, every morning and night
we brush our teeth so we don't get sugar bugs.
But they are very sneaky!"

"Like wayyyy back here?!"
Nora said pointing to the back of her mouth.

"I know!" cheered Nora as she raced to her room.
When she returned,
she had her friend Rosie a bright red teddy bear.

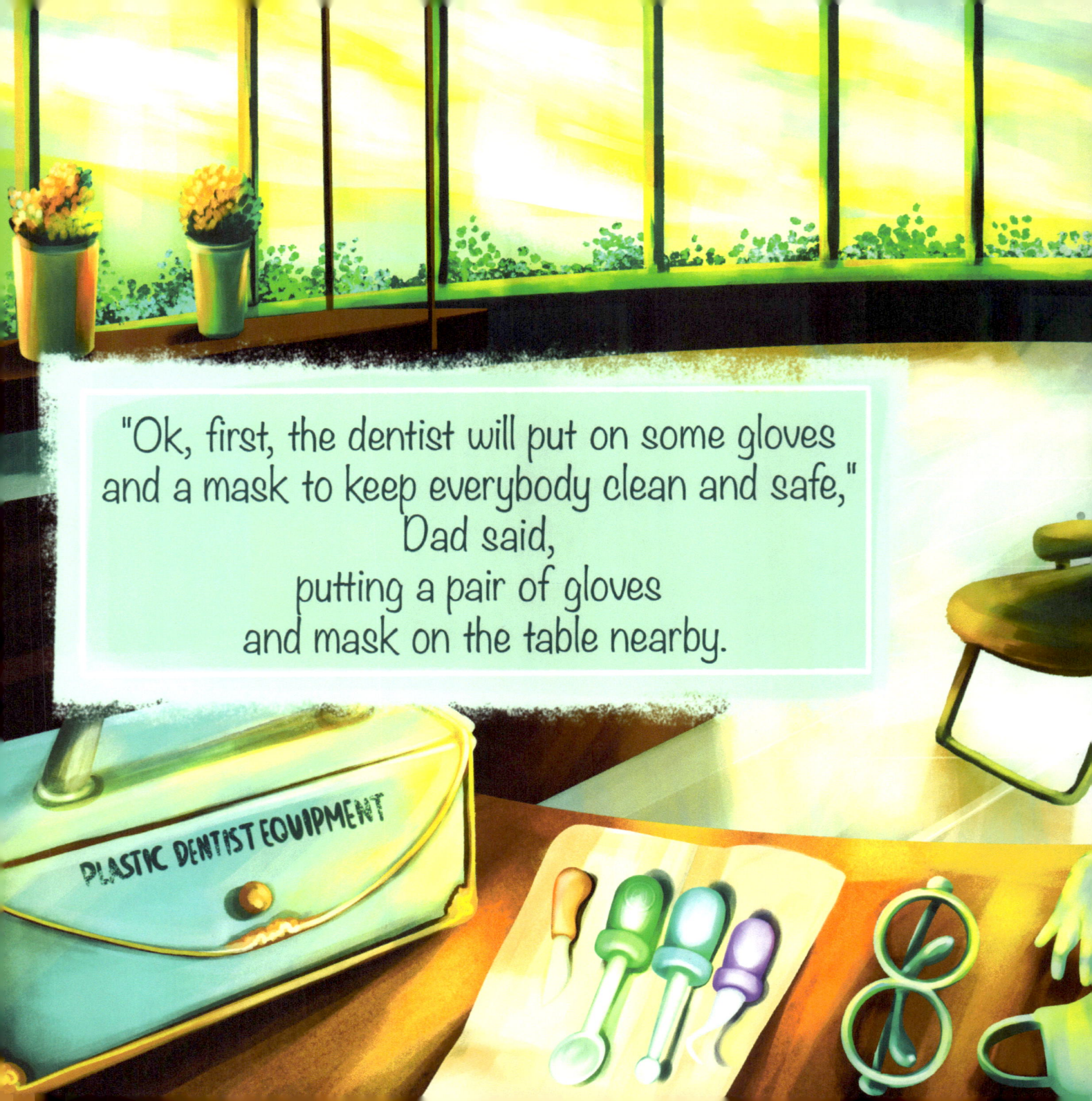

"Ok, first, the dentist will put on some gloves and a mask to keep everybody clean and safe," Dad said,
putting a pair of gloves and mask on the table nearby.

"Next, you will wear some glasses to protect your eyes from the light. And a paper bib to keep you clean. Here is a pair for Rosie too!" Said Dad.

"The chair at the dentist will move.
It's no big deal, though!
It's like a ride at the park!" Dad said.

"Next, the dentist will use a special tool to count your teeth. First, it's your turn. Then it's Rosie's turn!" Dad said with a smile.

"First,
the bottom 1 2 3 4 5 6 7 8 9 10,"
Dad said calmly.

"Now the top 1 2 3 4 5 6 7 8 9 10," he said excitedly.
"good job sitting so still!".

"Now it's Rosie's turn!" cheered Nora. "1 2 3 4 5 6 7 8 9 10"

"Now, we will use this tool to check your gums. It will touch your cheek, and I will count to 3"

"Next comes the x-rays!" Dad says. "They help the dentists to see between the teeth where we can not see with our eyes!!"

"Sugar bugs like to hide !!
That is why we floss between our teeth
where the toothbrush can not go!!"

"We will put this in your mouth until the timer is finished. Now, copy me!" said Dad.

"And a heavy jacket, right dad?"
Nora said with a sigh.
"That's right."
Said dad. "I will set a timer so
you know how long until you can take it off."

"After the X-rays,
the dentist will polish your teeth
with their polisher." Said dad.

"And remember if there is a silly taste it's no big deal; you can close your lips on the little vacuum to get rid of the taste at any time." said Dad. "Just put your hand up and the dentist will use the vacuum"

"I remember, the vacuum feels funny!!", said Nora

"Then,
they will floss to clean the hiding places between the teeth!!"
Dad said.

"We floss at home too!" said Nora. "That's right!" said Dad. "Sugar Bugs are tricky hiders, but we are better seekers!!"

"Once your teeth are clean, the dentist will make them nice and strong with Tooth Vitamins called Fluoride." Said Dad. "They will paint it on. It tastes a little different, but you can choose a flavour!"

"What happens if they find sugar bugs?" Nora asked.
"It's no big deal." Said Dad.
"If the dentist finds Sugar bugs hiding in your teeth, we will go back a different day to catch them!!" said dad.

"The dentist will spray them to sleep and brush them out of the hole they have made and give you a nice new filling that makes your tooth very special."

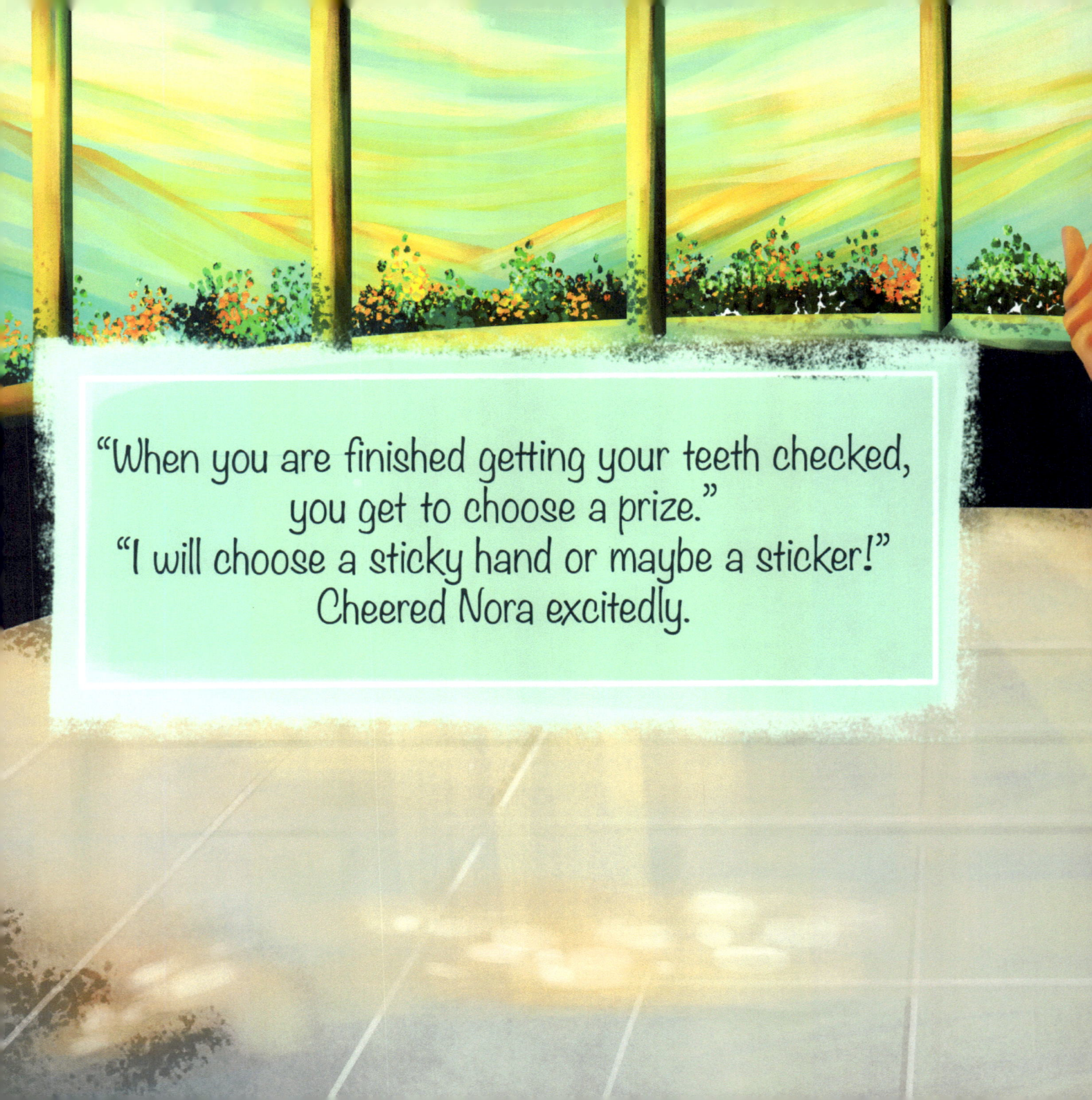

"When you are finished getting your teeth checked, you get to choose a prize."
"I will choose a sticky hand or maybe a sticker!" Cheered Nora excitedly.

"Then it's Rosie's turn, ahhh…."
Nora cheered

"Yay!" cheered Nora. "I chose a red sticky hand just like Rosie!"

"Great job today! You were very patient during your visit today." Dad said proudly. "Here are some special prizes for you to choose from!"

Dentists Are No Big Deal

Dear Caregivers of young children,
Thank you for taking care of your child's teeth!

We need their help! They have to trust us that we are there to help them. They have to open wide and stay still. We will explain everything to them. It is our goal to make this a life long positive experience for them.

Most young children have no experience with dental treatment. They get information from other people — good and bad. It is up to you what words you would like the child to know but in my 25 plus years of experience if they know they are getting a needle they become fearful right away. As no one likes needles. We generally use other terms to explain how the anesthetic is administered. "sleepy juice that sprays everything to sleep" "the Sugar Bug might bite like a mosquito"

I hope that this book will help explain some of the steps and tools used to do a dental filling.

Please work with the Dental Team and make this the start of many years of happy dental health for your child.

Yours in Good Dental Health,
Debbie Kesslering

No Big Deals

Hey there, friend! Do you ever feel nervous or scared about doing things like getting a haircut or going to the dentist? It's totally normal to feel that way, but it's important to practice those tricky self-care tasks so we can take good care of ourselves.

One way to practice is by starting with "No Big Deals." Getting a haircut can be a big deal for many people. If sitting in a chair is "No Big Deal" then that is a great place to start! By breaking these big skills down into smaller skills, we can celebrate each step until things like haircuts become "No Big Deal." This takes time, though! So the key is to practice!

Remember, it's okay to feel scared or nervous sometimes, but we don't want those feelings to stop us from taking care of ourselves. By practicing these steps, we can overcome those tricky tasks and feel proud of ourselves for taking care of our bodies and minds. Keep up the good work!

Strategies for No Big Deals

- Practice, Practice, Practice!
- Use visual timers or tokens to make expectations clear.
- Allow for frequent breaks to keep everyone successful.
- Use "first", "then" statements and keep things **positive**!
    - "First sit in the chair, then we can choose your show!"